CREATIVE COMPANIES

THE STORY OF FACEBOOK

SARA GILBERT

JAICO PUBLISHING HOUSE

Ahmedabad Bangalore Chennai
Delhi Hyderabad Kolkata Mumbai

Published by Jaico Publishing House
A-2 Jash Chambers, 7-A Sir Phirozshah Mehta Road
Fort, Mumbai - 400 001
jaicopub@jaicobooks.com
www.jaicobooks.com

Published in arrangement with
The Creative Company
123 South Broad Street, Mankato, MN 56001, USA

To be sold only in India, Bangladesh, Bhutan,
Pakistan, Nepal, Sri Lanka and the Maldives.

Design by Zeno Design
Production by Christine Vanderbeek
Art Direction by Rita Marshall

Photographs by Alamy (Art Directors & TRIP, CJG-Technology, digitallife, NetPhotos, NetPics), Corbis (Rick Friedman, PHILMcCARTEN/Reuters, BRIAN SNYDER/Reuters, Wu Kaixiang/XinHua/Xinhua Press), Getty Images (Antoine Antoniol/Bloomberg , Juana Arias/The Washington Post, Tony Avelar/Bloomberg, Noah Berger/Bloomberg, Andrew Harrer/Bloomberg, Gilles Mingasson, Leon Neal/AFP, Justin Sullivan, Kimberly White)

THE STORY OF FACEBOOK
ISBN 978-81-8495-438-8

First Jaico Impression: 2013
12th Jaico Impression: 2025

Page design and layouts: Special Effects, Mumbai

Printed by
Trinity Academy For Corporate Training Limited, Mumbai

CREATIVE COMPANIES

THE STORY OF FACEBOOK

facebook
Facebook helps you connect and share with the people in your life.

On the afternoon of February 4, 2004, Mark Zuckerberg sat down at his desk in the suite he shared with three other Harvard University students. A few weeks earlier, the 19-year-old student had registered the domain name for a new Web site. He had spent his entire winter break hunched over his computer in his dorm room, designing an online social network for fellow students. Now he was finally ready to launch the new site. As his computer hummed to life amidst the empty energy drink cans and crumpled food wrappers, Zuckerberg prepared to click the final button that would make Thefacebook.com live—and that would start a web of connections that quickly crisscrossed the campus, the country, and then the globe.

1

College Connections

Mark Zuckerberg arrived at Harvard University in 2002 with a reputation as a computer whiz. He had been writing code since he was about 10 years old, when he developed games to play on his parents' home computer.

In high school, he worked with a friend to create a software program that personalized music play-lists according to a listener's preferences. Microsoft had reportedly offered almost $1 million for the technology—and Zuckerberg and his friend had turned it down, a fact that was well known among students on Harvard's Cambridge, Massachusetts, campus.

Zuckerberg, a computer science major, wasn't interested in programming to get rich. It was a hobby, something that came naturally to the gifted youngster and that attracted attention on campus. Students appreciated the Course Match site he developed as a sophomore because it allowed them to select their classes based on the other students already enrolled in them so that they could be with friends. The Facemash site he created that same year, however, was not so widely adored. The site placed photos of Harvard students side by side and asked viewers to rank them according to looks. After launching Facemash, Zuckerberg was summoned before the university's administrative board and put on probation for hacking into the university's systems to obtain the photos.

Not long after the Facemash controversy, Zuckerberg became consumed by another programming project: an online social network that would allow Harvard students to connect with each other. Although his motives were primarily social, Zuckerberg recognized that this new Web site had the potential to become a business that might eventually generate a little income as well. To help him stay on top of the business aspects, Zuckerberg partnered with business major Eduardo Saverin, who matched Zuckerberg's investment of $1,000 to pay for the servers needed to host the site and also provided financial advice along the way.

Zuckerberg named the site Thefacebook.com, after the online photo collections for each residence hall at Harvard, which the students called "facebooks." The only requirement for registration on the site was an active Harvard e-mail address. Users created profile pages that included a photo and personal information—whether they were

Mark Zuckerberg, pictured here at Harvard in May 2004,
was born and raised in New York

single or in a relationship, for example, as well as lists of their favorite books, movies, musical groups, and more. Each user could invite other students to be their "friends" on Thefacebook and could limit who would be able to view the information they posted on their page.

Almost as soon as Thefacebook went live on February 4, 2004, several dozen students who heard about it from friends signed up. Four days later, more than 650 students were using the site. Thefacebook became one of the hottest topics around campus. Within three weeks, it had 6,000 users—including undergraduate and graduate students, alumni, faculty, and staff.

The task of working out the kinks of Thefacebook's design and keeping its rapid growth from crashing the servers quickly became overwhelming. Zuckerberg hired one of his roommates, Dustin Moskovitz, to help him keep up. Although Zuckerberg couldn't pay Moskovitz cash, he promised him a 5 percent ownership stake in the site; as the creator, Zuckerberg held 65 percent,

Eight days younger than Zuckerberg,
Dustin Moskovitz (pictured) helped design the Facebook site

and Saverin held 30 percent.

While Zuckerberg's time was spent tweaking Thefacebook's code and making it run smoothly, Moskovitz's role was handling requests from students at other schools wanting access to Thefacebook. The site went live at Columbia University on February 25; it was launched at Stanford University the next day and Yale University three days later, connecting students at the various schools with one another. The immediate popularity of the social network at those schools prompted a reporter from the *Stanford Daily* to interview Zuckerberg about his intentions with Thefacebook.com. "I know it sounds corny," he said. "But I'd love to improve people's lives, especially socially."

> *"Part of our company mission was to be the coolest company in Silicon Valley. I played up the idea that this should be a fun, rock-'n'-roll place to work."*
>
> Sean Parker,
> Former Facebook President

Facebook's California headquarters have always been known for their youthful, laid-back atmosphere

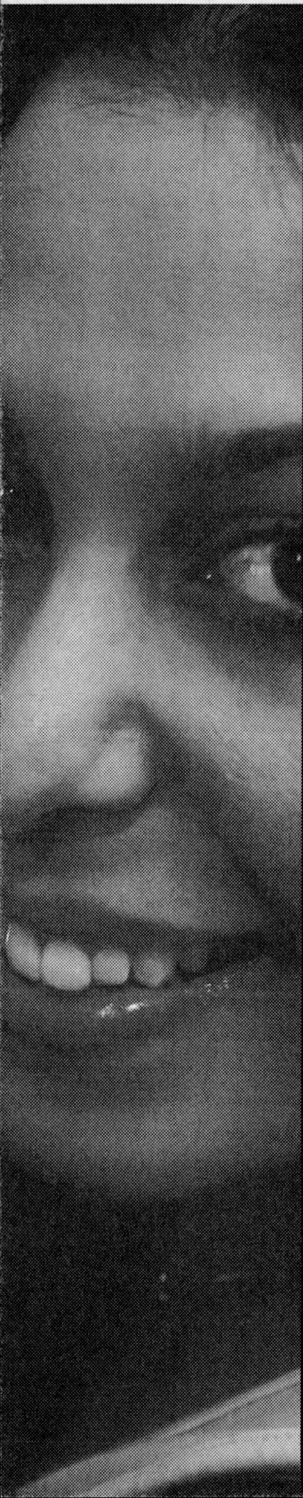

From Friendster to Facebook

Although Facebook has become the world's most widely used social networking site, it certainly wasn't the first. Almost 10 years before Mark Zuckerberg launched Thefacebook in 2004, Match.com started helping people find dates, and Classmates.com started helping people connect with former school friends in 1995. Although neither of those sites were much like modern social networks, they initiated the idea that people could connect with each other online. In 1997, a site called Sixdegrees.com took the idea further, attempting to build a network based on shared relationships among users. But it was the social networking site Friendster, which launched in 2003, that caught Zuckerberg's attention—and that focused his mission for Facebook. One of the lessons he learned from Friendster was to invest adequately in servers to keep the site running. Friendster had notoriously slow servers that often crashed, which led to its ultimate demise.

When calls from reporters started coming more often, Zuckerberg recruited his more articulate roommate, Chris Hughes, to serve as Thefacebook's official spokesperson. Hughes reiterated a point Zuckerberg made often: the goal was not to make money on the site but to provide a fun and worthwhile service to students.

But as Thefacebook spread from campus to campus and registered users grew to more than 30,000 by the end of March, Zuckerberg realized that he would have to find some source of revenue to offset the ballooning costs of running the business. Thefacebook was paying $450 a month for the 5 servers it required to stay up and running, and more servers would certainly be needed in the near future. Saverin started selling a few ads that began appearing on Thefacebook in April and invested another $10,000 in the company. Zuckerberg, meanwhile, fielded calls from people who wanted to invest in the site—including an offer to purchase the 4-month-old business for $10 million.

Zuckerberg wasn't interested. In 6 months,

Thefacebook had spread to 34 campuses and had accumulated 100,000 users. He was so committed to the site and its growth that he decided to move to northern California's Silicon Valley, a longtime hotbed for technology startups, over the summer. "[It] was kind of this mythical place where all the techs used to come from," he told a reporter. "So I was like, I want to check that out."

2

Five Million Friends

Zuckerberg, Moskovitz, and two interns rented a house in Palo Alto for the summer of 2004. They had no car and very little furniture. Their dining room table was piled high with computers, modems, and cameras, as well as empty bottles and soda cans. Like many college students, they avoided early mornings. Often they'd start working in the afternoon and keep at it until well after midnight.

They had another collaborator working with them as well: Sean Parker, who had been involved with the online music sharing service Napster as well as other Internet ventures. Parker admired the concept behind Thefacebook and immediately liked Zuckerberg, whom he had met at a dinner in New York earlier that year. Although Parker had yet to turn 25 years old, he became the oldest and most experienced member of Thefacebook's team when he joined the operation during the summer of 2004.

Zuckerberg, Moskovitz, and the interns spent their time improving Thefacebook .com, bolstering its servers, and writing computer code for new features and services, including ways for users to send private messages to each other. Parker, meanwhile, devoted much of his time to helping Thefacebook become a bona fide business. He had become acquainted with a network of potential investors during his time with other Internet companies, and he approached them again for Thefacebook.

Zuckerberg still wasn't sure that he wanted to invite investors into the business, and he didn't want to rely too heavily on advertising, either. But Thefacebook was going to need more funds than the tiny amount trickling in from advertisers. Zuckerberg had already spent almost $20,000 on new equipment, primarily servers. "I need servers just as much as I need food," Zuckerberg said that summer. "I could probably go a while without eating, but if we don't have enough servers then the site is screwed."

By the end of the summer, the site's 200,000 users were straining the company's infrastructure. So in the fall of 2004, Parker arranged a meeting with Peter Thiel, the cofounder of the secure online payment system known as PayPal, who was now privately investing in Internet startups. Even though Zuckerberg wore a T-shirt, jeans, and rubber flip-flops—his usual outfit—to the meeting, Thiel was impressed by both the young chief executive officer (CEO) and Thefacebook site. He offered a loan of $500,000, which would

Like Zuckerberg, Sean Parker (pictured) was a computer genius, having done programming since age six eventually give him a 10 percent stake in the company. A handful of other private investors contributed another $100,000 to the company's resources.

That infusion of cash convinced Zuckerberg and Moskovitz not to return to Harvard in the fall. Instead, they moved into an office above a Chinese restaurant on Emerson Street in Palo Alto, hired artists to paint colorful murals on the walls, and bought cheap furniture that they had to put together themselves. They also introduced a pair of new features for users. The first was a "wall" where friends could post comments and notes. The second was

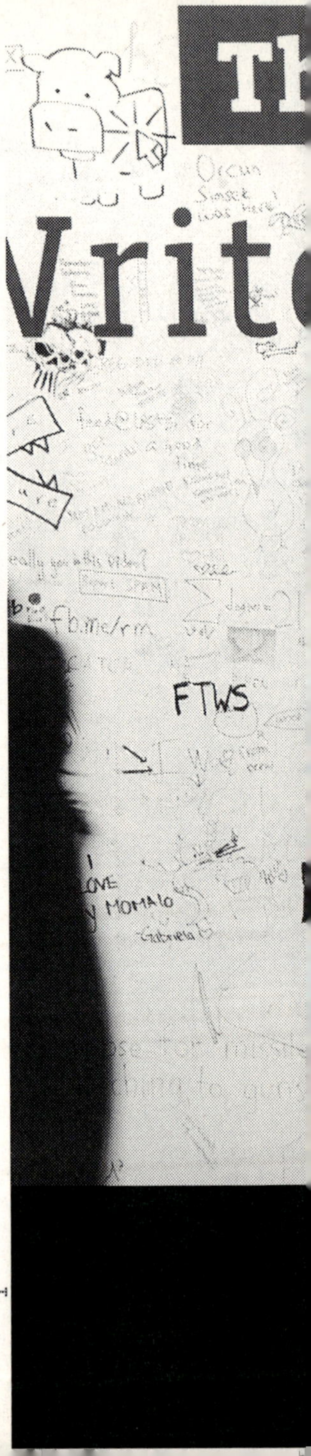

From its earliest days, Facebook invited user suggestions,
as on this scribble board in Palo Alto

the Groups function, which allowed users to unite around any common bond, from classes they were taking to beverages they enjoyed. Membership grew to 400,000 in September and then to 500,000 in October. The one-millionth user registered on November 30.

In the face of such rapid growth, Zuckerberg and his team realized that the $600,000 they had received wasn't going to last very long. Private investors and venture capital firms (which give large sums of money to new and emerging companies in exchange for an ownership stake) began calling Zuckerberg. He was surprised when one company offered to buy Thefacebook outright for $75 million. But after months of evaluating competing offers, in May 2005, Zuckerberg accepted $12.7 million from the venture capital company Accel Partners. In return, Accel Partners received 15 percent ownership of the company, which officially became known as simply Facebook a few months later.

The new investment meant that Zuckerberg

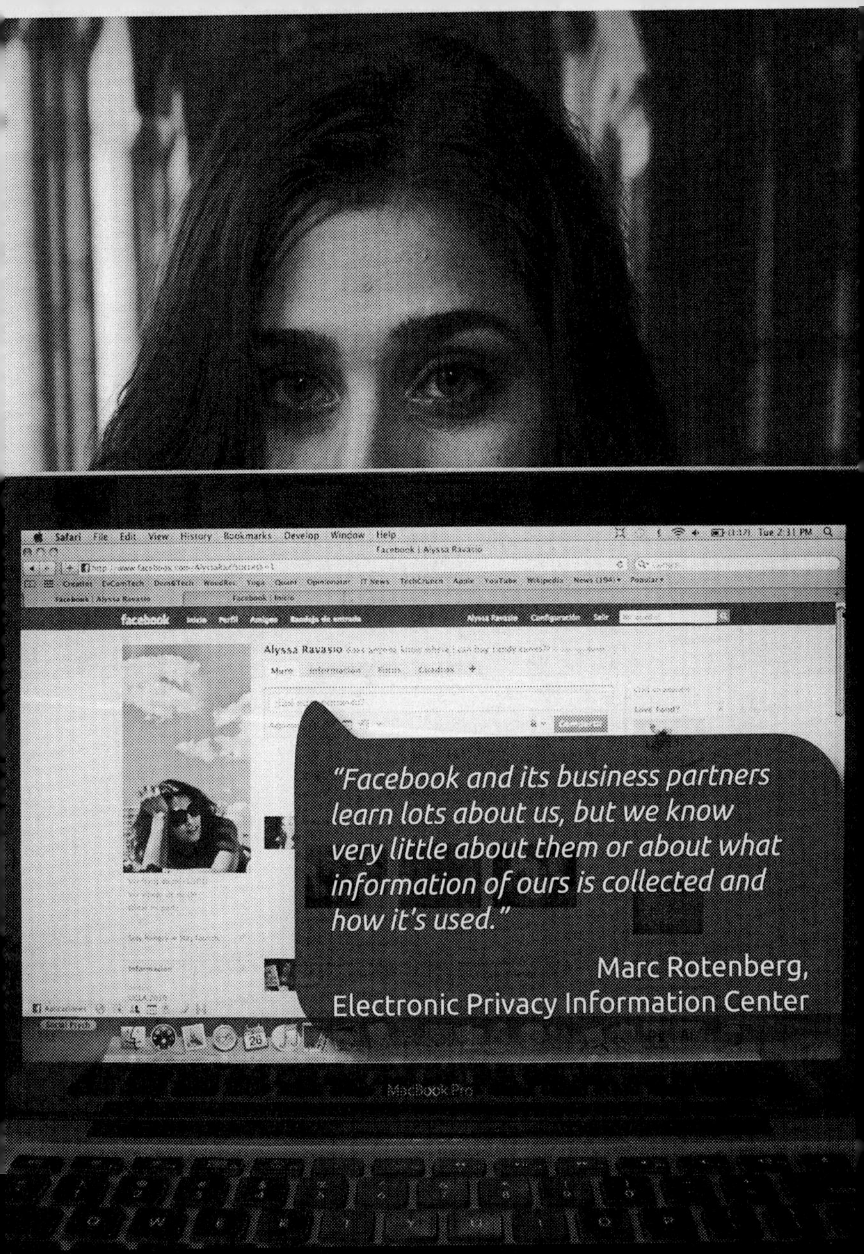

"Facebook and its business partners learn lots about us, but we know very little about them or about what information of ours is collected and how it's used."

Marc Rotenberg,
Electronic Privacy Information Center

Facebook competed with—and eventually beat out—another social networking site called Myspace.

Legal Wrangling

Before Facebook had been around for a full year, its founder was hit with a lawsuit related to the site. It came from three fellow Harvard students who, in 2003, had asked for Zuckerberg's help designing a dating and socializing Web site they planned to call Harvard Connection. Zuckerberg agreed to join the crew but later bowed out, saying he was too busy to continue working on it. When Facebook launched shortly after that, the students—twins Cameron and Tyler Winklevoss and Divya Narendra—claimed Zuckerberg had stolen their idea, and they decided to challenge him in court. Zuckerberg shrugged it off, saying the sites were "completely different" and calling their threats "ridiculous." He hired lawyers to fight the charges, including copyright infringement, and settled the suit with a $20-million cash payment and Facebook stock to Narendra and the Winklevoss brothers in 2008. Although they accepted the settlement, the Winklevoss brothers attempted to reopen the case in 2010.

could upgrade his growing network of servers. It also meant that he could start hiring more people to help build and maintain the site. He planted a wooden menu board on the sidewalk in front the office building, with positions such as vice president of engineering advertised in chalk. Eventually, Facebook also hired a recruiter to find and hire engineers so that Zuckerberg could focus his own efforts on the bigger-picture needs of Facebook.

One of the issues on his mind was expanding Facebook. By the fall of 2005, the site was operating at more than 1,800 colleges and universities. At least 85 percent of the college students in the United States were registered users, and more than half of them visited the site daily. Zuckerberg was eager to reach new demographics, and he believed that high school students were a natural next step.

In September, Facebook officially invited high school students to register on the site—but there was a catch. Because few high schools issue e-mail addresses to all students, as most colleges do, Facebook couldn't verify the identities of individuals. The solution was for registered college users to invite their younger friends to join Facebook; those new members could then invite their friends, and so on. By the following spring, more than 1 million of the 5.5 million active "Facebookers" were high school students.

3

Growing Pains

Barely two years into its existence, Facebook was undeniably successful, not only in the U.S. and Canada, but also in the United Kingdom, where the service was now available. The photo application it had launched in late 2005, which allowed users to post photos to the site and share them with friends, had been a huge hit. But Facebook was still burning through millions of dollars just to maintain its servers and upgrade its technology.

Although suitors continued to call with offers to buy the company, Zuckerberg resisted. He did begin to think more seriously about allowing advertisements to be displayed alongside the information on a user's page, something he had opposed in the past. But if they could help fund continued expansion, he was now willing to consider small, well-placed ads that didn't distract from Facebook's content. Most of the early advertising was customized; companies created sponsored groups for certain products and paid Facebook according to how many users signed up. Proctor & Gamble, for example, created a "Smile State" group promoting Crest White Strips—and promised free movie tickets to anyone who joined the group.

More than 20,000 people did. Zuckerberg appreciated advertising that allowed companies to connect with customers without actually running banner ads on the pages—but he turned down $1 million from Sprite to turn Facebook's homepage green for a day to promote the soft drink.

Meanwhile, Facebook's engineers were planning to reach out to a new audience again. Zuckerberg had decided that workplaces, where most adult social interaction occurs, should be the next frontier, so in May 2006, Facebook launched work networks to connect adults with others in their workplaces. But to his surprise, work networks flopped. Few, if any, people signed up, in part because there had been little advanced marketing. Zuckerberg was crushed, and a black cloud hung over the office. "It was the most wrong he'd ever been at Facebook, and the first time he'd ever been wrong in a big way," said Matt Cohler, one of Zuckerberg's closest advisers in the company.

That disappointment was muted by the August announcement of a strategic relationship with software maker Microsoft to develop and sell banner ads for the site, which Zuckerberg had agreed to accept. That partnership opened up a lucrative advertising stream that immediately turned 2006 into the company's first profitable

Facebook's photo application became hugely popular, allowing for quick and easy image sharing year. With his confidence restored, Zuckerberg prepared to launch two of the company's biggest initiatives in September 2006.

The first was News Feed, which would collect the most recent and relevant information about each user's friends and create a scrolling News Feed screen for the user to view. When a friend uploaded new photos, changed a piece of information, or updated his or her status, it would appear on the News Feed screen. It was a complex project that had the potential to revolutionize the way users interacted. No longer would they have to click on their friends' pages to see what they were doing; News Feed brought the information to them.

The second project was

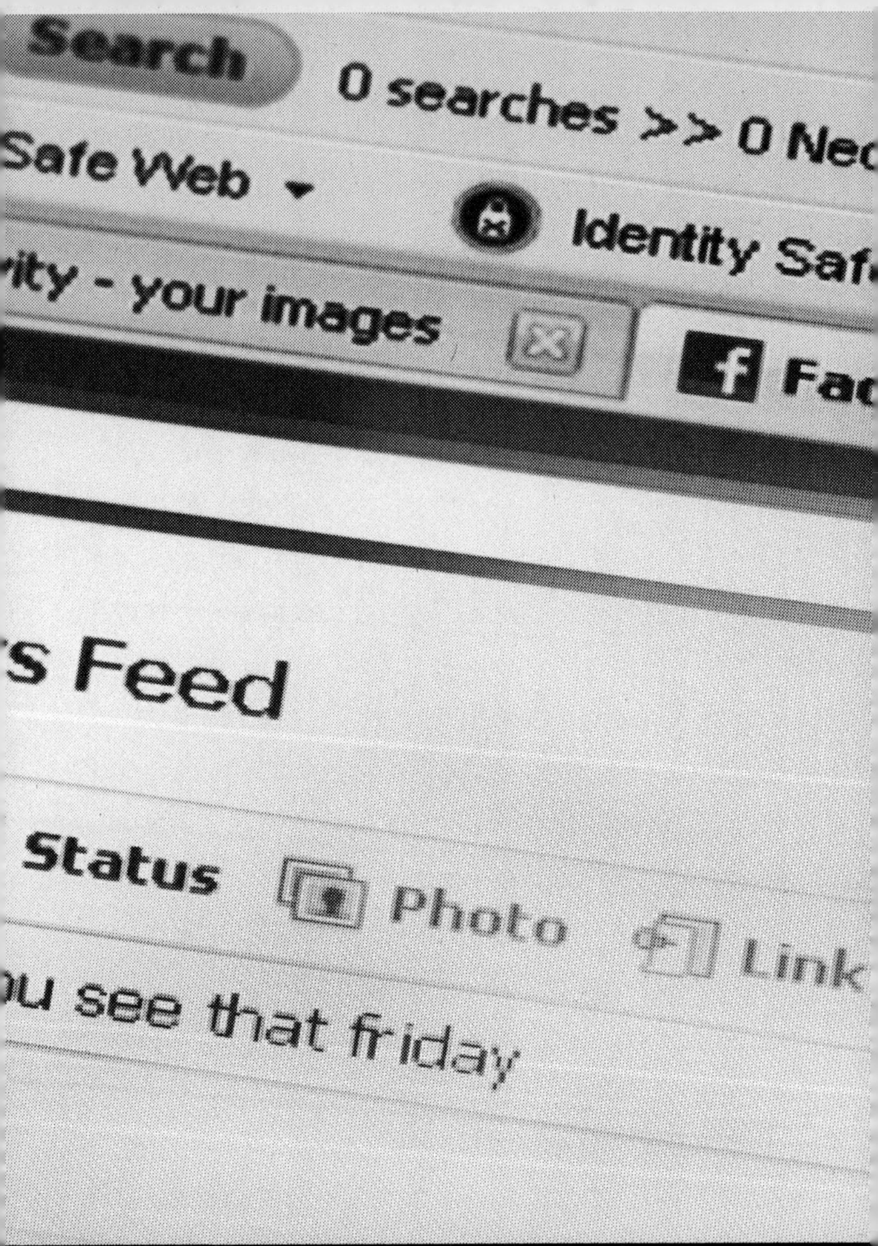

Facebook's News Feed feature was designed
to simplify the user experience but quickly created controversy

another attempt to broaden Facebook's audience. Zuckerberg remained convinced that Facebook could be a tool for people of all ages to connect with friends and had decided that "open registration," which would make the site available to anyone, anywhere, would begin in the fall. As one team of engineers worked day and night preparing for the launch of News Feed, another team created a service to help open registration users find friends based on names in their e-mail address books.

News Feed launched early in the morning of September 5. But as the Facebook team swigged champagne directly from the bottle in celebration, users started complaining in Facebook posts and e-mails that the new format was an invasion of their privacy. They begged for it to be turned off. One user created a group called "Students Against Facebook News Feed," which had more than 100,000 members within 24 hours.

The staff was dumbfounded. The information available through News Feed had previously been

"I want everybody here to be careful about what you post on Facebook, because in the YouTube [Internet video] age, whatever you do will be pulled up later somewhere in your life."

U.S. President Barack Obama

Politicians—including U.S. president Barack Obama—came to recognize Facebook's growing influence

Person
Facebook's
Mark
Zuckerberg
THE CONNECTOR
Facebook's
Mark
Zuckerberg
THE CONNECTOR

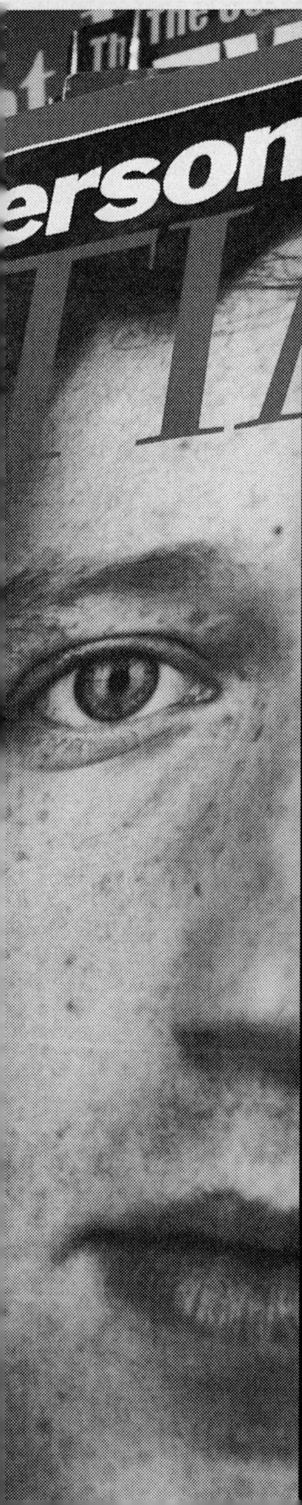

Celebrity Status

Mark Zuckerberg has garnered a reputation for being shy, soft-spoken, and intensely private about his personal life—and the fame and notoriety he's earned as Facebook's founder hasn't changed him. Even after his company had made him a billionaire, he was most commonly seen wearing the shorts, hooded sweatshirt, and flip-flop sandals that he had preferred as a college student. But his celebrity status came with a price. Zuckerberg became so recognizable that people often interrupted him at restaurants and other public places to ask for an autograph or a picture with him. Such intrusions became more common after a movie about Facebook was released in 2010. The Social Network was one of the most popular movies of the year, but Zuckerberg was not among its fans. "I started Facebook to improve the world and make it a more transparent place, and this movie portrays me as someone who built Facebook so I could meet girls," he said.

available to users' friends anyway. News Feed just made access to updates easier and more immediate. But Zuckerberg remained remarkably calm. He saw the viral response to News Feed's release as evidence that it was effective, since users were taking advantage of the feature to spread their opinions about it. He knew, however, that the company had to respond. So he instituted new privacy features that would give users control over what information was posted on the News Feed. Then he sent a message to Facebook users: "We really messed this one up," he wrote, apologizing for not better preparing them for the new features. He explained what the company was doing in response to their complaints. And just as quickly as it had started, the anti-News Feed movement fizzled out.

Now the Facebook staff prepared for the September 26 beginning of open registration. But instead of sipping champagne immediately, they spent the first two weeks after the launch huddled anxiously over data about new users, looking for some indication of success. By early October, they had it. New users were joining at a rate of 50,000 per day—a significant increase over the 20,000 per day prior to open registration and an indication that adults were eagerly signing up for the service.

4

More than Friends

The 22-year-old Zuckerberg bused all 150 Facebook employees to California's Great America theme park in Santa Clara for a holiday party at the end of 2006. But when they returned to the company's offices, which were now scattered throughout several buildings located on Palo Alto's University Avenue, it was time to get serious about business.

Facebook was being used by more than 12 million people around the world, a number that grew by the tens of thousands daily. But there was still plenty of additional work to be done.

Zuckerberg knew that Facebook's photo application wasn't perfect; the photos weren't high resolution, and the printing function didn't work well. He also knew that a new event invitation function, which would allow users to notify their friends about upcoming activities in which they might be interested, was extremely basic. Even so, both photos and events were incredibly popular on Facebook—proof that users weren't looking for sophisticated software as much as functional connections with their friends.

That realization helped push the next big idea for Facebook, one that Zuckerberg had been obsessing about since the company's earliest days: becoming a platform on which other software applications could be built and run. His roots as a programmer fueled his desire to open the door for other aspiring engineers and software designers to create new applications for Facebook users. He assumed that the web of connections between those users would allow the best applications to spread rapidly throughout the network.

Zuckerberg was so excited about the idea that he hired an event planner to prepare a glitzy launch party. On the day of the party, more than 750 people—including journalists and representatives from software and Internet companies—packed into a hotel ballroom. "Together, we're starting a movement," Zuckerberg told the crowd. Then he demonstrated how the new Facebook platform could be used to create applications. Afterward, he invited developers to join him for an eight-hour, hands-on software development session in which participants had the opportunity to begin working on actual applications (or apps, as they became known). The immediate reactions were overwhelmingly positive. Six months after the launch, more than 250,000 developers

Palo Alto is a city of fewer than 70,000,
but it looms large as a hot spot for technology companies

were operating 25,000 approved applications on Facebook, from the Graffiti app that let users "scribble" notes on their friends' pages to poker and word games. Zuckerberg particularly enjoyed a Scrabble-like game that helped him convince his grandparents to join Facebook and play it with him online.

Facebook Platform elevated the company's standing as a technology company, not just a media company. It gave many of its users a reason to visit more often and to stay on the site longer. And it helped turn many of the small developers who were contributing applications into prosperous businesses, since they were able to either charge for use of their apps or to sell advertising alongside them.

Facebook's "Lexulous" game was originally called "Scrabulous," but a lawsuit forced a name change

But Facebook, meanwhile, was again in need of more money. As the site grew to more than 50 million users in the fall of 2007, half of whom lived outside the U.S., the challenge to build and maintain a suitable infrastructure grew, too.

The first thought was to seek out new investors interested in owning a small stake in the company—and many were, thanks to the glow surrounding Facebook in light of its international growth and the success of its platform. Among those eager to invest were both Google and Microsoft, rival companies who also wanted to negotiate advertising rights for the site. In October, a deal with Microsoft was announced that surprised many observers because of its size: Microsoft invested $240 million in Facebook in exchange for 1.6 percent of the company.

Facebook's financial outlook brightened again in November, when Zuckerberg announced Facebook Ads, an advertising system that he was more comfortable incorporating into the site. Businesses could build pages and seek Facebook

"Our mission since day one has been to make society more open.... We help people be more open across more contexts."

Dave Morin,
Longtime Facebook Employee

Although Facebook aspired to draw users of all ages, most of its users—and employees—were young

Tools
Barack Obama | Facebook
facebook
Sign Up
Barack Obama is on Faceboo
Sign up for Facebook to connec
This page is run by Organizing for
America, the grassroots organization
for President Obama's agenda for
change. To visit the White House
page, go to

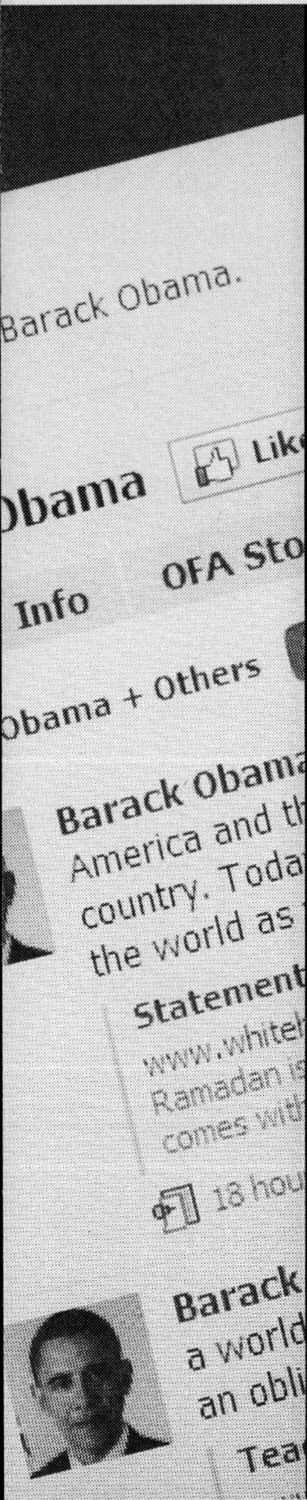

Politically Involved

From the beginning, Facebook users proudly posted their political beliefs on the site. Eventually, the politicians they often wrote about began to create their own Facebook pages as well. In 2008, Facebook became a prominent venue for discussion among its members and the candidates running for office—including the two major presidential candidates, senators John McCain and Barack Obama. Obama strategically hired Chris Hughes, one of the original Facebook founders, to help run the online component of his campaign for president. With Hughes's help, Obama created a strong following on Facebook, amassing more than a million friends during the course of the campaign. In the process, he extended his message to a younger audience that didn't always pay attention to traditional media outlets. The strategy worked; Obama received almost 70 percent of the vote among Americans younger than 25 in what became known to many observers as "the Facebook election."

"fans." Individuals signed up as fans of a particular company and in turn occasionally received special opportunities or timely information. The companies could also develop small ads that could be targeted to appear on the pages of specific user groups, based on users' ages, locations, and even products and services they had purchased. Facebook gathered all of that information through online tracking systems.

The use of such information, paired with a new Facebook application known as Beacon, became one of the company's worst blunders. Beacon inserted notes about purchases users made online into the News Feeds of friends. Not only did that feel like an invasion of privacy to many people, but it also spoiled surprises for others. A woman found out that she was getting a diamond ring for Christmas when a post on her Facebook News Feed noted that her husband had purchased one at Overstock.com.

Zuckerberg was surprised by the furor caused over Beacon. Once again, the Facebook CEO had to make a public apology about a problematic feature. “We simply did a bad job with this release,” he finally admitted as he announced that users could opt in or out of Beacon. “I apologize for it.”

5
Private Matters

Although some users were still angry with Facebook, the company decided to move forward with its plans for growth. Early in 2008, it made sites available in Spanish, French, and German for its European users. In April, it launched Facebook Chat, an instant-messaging format that allowed friends who were on Facebook at the same time to type instant messages to each other.

In the midst of all that, the privacy concerns that had been stirred up by the Beacon release were simmering in the background. Users were growing more and more alarmed by the amount of information Facebook knew about them and by who might have access to that information. In March, the company announced updated privacy controls that allowed users to decide how much of their information would be available to all Facebook users. They could also limit certain parts of their profiles to people who were registered as their friends or to anyone registered as a friend of one of their friends.

Although some within Facebook thought the controls should go further, Zuckerberg believed that people should be allowed and even encouraged to share information freely. He wrote frequently in blog posts that users should have a right to control their own information—but that he also envisioned a more open and transparent society in which more information would be public.

To that end, he introduced a new set of privacy controls late in 2009 and instructed all Facebook users to adjust their settings again. The new feature this time was an "everyone" option, which let users select certain pieces of information that they were willing to share with all of Facebook's 350 million users. In the process, however, Facebook made "everyone" the default for all information pending each user's adjustment. That meant that many Facebook members who weren't paying attention or who didn't take the time to check their privacy settings were suddenly more exposed than they realized. In addition, Facebook made all users' names, profile pictures, and genders publicly available by default. And then there were the random glitches that occasionally sent private messages to unintended recipients or that made private chats public.

Users were up in arms again—but they were not the only ones. In December 2009, a group of 10 privacy organizations jointly filed a formal complaint with the U.S. Federal Trade

As Facebook grew, it faced sporadic protests against the ways it collected and used personal data

Commission (FTC). They sought an investigation into Facebook's handling of information and wished to levy financial penalties against the company. By early 2010, four U.S. senators had joined the call as well, asking the FTC to set new privacy guidelines for Facebook and other social networking sites.

Despite his preference to be as open as possible, Zuckerberg had to address the complaints. He arranged meetings with privacy advocates and with New York senator Charles Schumer, one of the lawmakers who had called on the FTC to look into Facebook's practices. With their input, in May 2010 Facebook rolled out a redesigned privacy policy that simplified the choices and offered users more powerful controls over their own information. "When

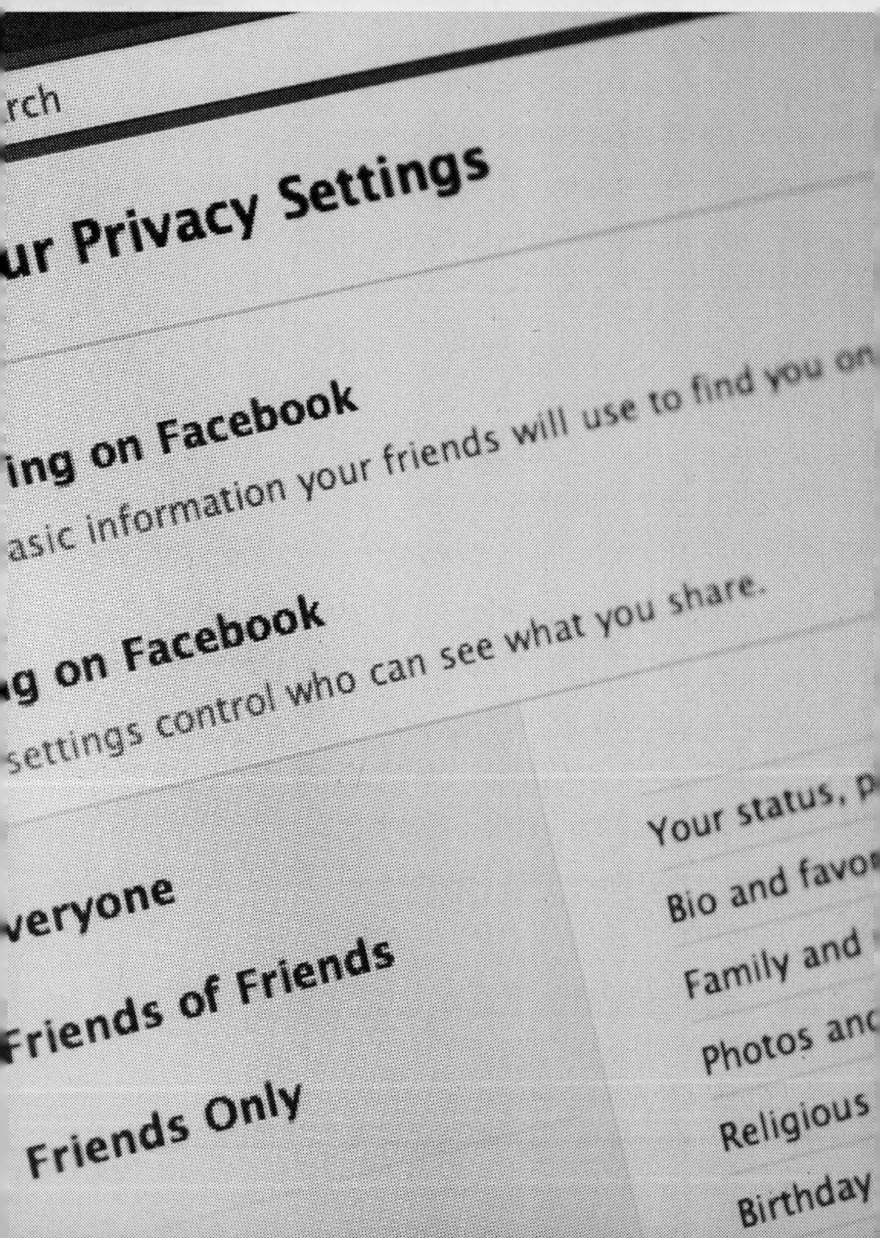

Facebook responded to user concerns by broadening the options for controlling the viewing of information people have control over what they share, they want to share more," he explained. "When people share more, the world becomes more open and connected.... The number one thing we've heard is that many users want a simpler way to control their information."

In early 2010, Facebook's membership numbered 400 million; by July, that figure had grown to 500 million—more than the populations of the U.S., Canada, and Mexico combined. Zuckerberg had moved the company's employees to a big, funky building in Palo Alto, where many of the walls and doors were giant white boards on which employees could scribble ideas and work out new plans. Breakfast was served to employees, who often rolled around the office on skateboards. The company's revenue was continuing to grow as well; in 2009, revenue was reportedly close to $700 million.

As a private company, Facebook wasn't required to release its financial information publicly. But by the end of 2010, many insiders,

By late 2011, Mark Zuckerberg, then 27, was one of the world's richest people, with $13.5 billion

Caught on Facebook

No matter how many privacy controls Facebook implemented, it couldn't stop people from posting things that might get them in trouble. Parents, schools, employers, and even law enforcement officials were all able to easily find incriminating evidence on the site. In one example, a high school student in Massachusetts combed through Facebook looking for pictures of classmates drinking and sent them to the principal. Another high school principal scanned through Facebook himself, looking for pictures of athletes at parties—and he suspended those he found holding bottles of beer. But it wasn't just kids getting in trouble: A young employee who told his boss that he needed to take time off because of a family crisis was busted when a friend posted a picture of him at a party on Facebook. And in New York, a police detective was demoted after posting a racially charged status update when Barack Obama was elected president.

including Peter Thiel, one of Facebook's first investors, were predicting that the company would eventually become a publicly held business with shares traded on the stock market. Everyone knew the timing would be up to Zuckerberg, who remained the CEO of Facebook and who controlled the largest block of stock in the company as well. Indeed, in February 2012, Zuckerberg announced that Facebook would go public and sell stock later in the year.

Zuckerberg had always been reluctant to discuss his financial goals for the company because he maintained that the money didn't matter as much as the benefits Facebook provided. But he didn't shy away from defining his future objectives for Facebook: to reach billions of users and to provide the best possible service to them.

Those are the same objectives Zuckerberg had for his social networking Web site when he launched it in his dorm room on a winter day in 2004. Although he may not have envisioned it growing to hundreds of millions of users around the world on that day, his intent to create connections among people and forge a more open atmosphere was the same then as it is now.

Glossary

advocates people or groups who support and defend a particular cause or interest

alumni a graduate or former student of a particular school

application a software program designed to help a user perform tasks, play games, or take other action on a computer or computerized device

blog an online journal with regular written entries and comments from readers

default a preselected option adopted by a computer program when no other alternative is specified by the user

demographics certain segments of the population identified by statistics such as age or income, usually for advertising purposes

domain name the words or symbols that serve as an address for a computer network or Web site

engineering a profession in which people design or build computer systems to solve problems

hacking gaining access to a computer or information on a computer without permission

infrastructure the underlying foundation and framework of an organization or company, which includes its employees and leaders as well as buildings and equipment

infringement an encroachment on or limitation of the rights of another person

interns advanced students or graduates who work, with supervision, in a professional position to gain experience in a certain field

marketing the process of promoting products or services

platform the base from which new computer programs and applications can be built and operated

probation a period of time during which a person's actions are closely monitored to ensure that no rules are broken

profitable making more money than is spent

resolution the degree of detail visible in a photographic, television, or screen image

revenue the money earned by a company; another word for income

servers the main computers in a network, or group of linked computers, on which shared programs and files are stored

shares the equal parts a company may be divided into; shareholders each hold a certain number of shares, or a percentage, of the company

social network a group of people linked in an online setting by common ties, such as friendship, employment, or other affiliations

software written programs or rules that control a computer's operations

startups companies that are in the early stages of operation

stock shared ownership in a company by many people who buy shares, or portions, of stock, hoping the company will make a profit and the stock value will increase

viral spreading from person to person rapidly, especially online

Selected Bibliography

Facebook. "Company Timeline." Facebook Press Room. http://www.facebook.com/press/info.php?timeline.

Geller, Adam. "Facebook Founder's Story No Longer His Alone." *The Associated Press,* Oct. 2, 2010.

Grossman, Lev. "Person of the Year 2010: Mark Zuckerberg." *TIME,* December 15, 2010.

Kirkpatrick, David. *The Facebook Effect.* New York: Simon & Schuster, 2010.

Mezrich, Ben. *The Accidental Billionaires.* New York: Doubleday, 2009.

The Social Network. DVD. Directed by David Fincher. 2010. Los Angeles: Sony Pictures, 2011.

Vascellaro, Jessica. "Facebook Grapples with Privacy Issues." May 19, 2010.

Index

JAICO PUBLISHING HOUSE

Elevate Your Life. Transform Your World.

ESTABLISHED IN 1946, Jaico Publishing House is home to world-transforming authors such as Sri Sri Paramahansa Yogananda, Osho, The Dalai Lama, Sri Sri Ravi Shankar, Sadhguru, Robin Sharma, Deepak Chopra, Jack Canfield, Eknath Easwaran, Devdutt Pattanaik, Khushwant Singh, John Maxwell, Brian Tracy and Stephen Hawking.

Our late founder Mr. Jaman Shah first established Jaico as a book distribution company. Sensing that independence was around the corner, he aptly named his company Jaico ('Jai' means victory in Hindi). In order to service the significant demand for affordable books in a developing nation, Mr. Shah initiated Jaico's own publications. Jaico was India's first publisher of paperback books in the English language.

While self-help, religion and philosophy, mind/body/spirit, and business titles form the cornerstone of our non-fiction list, we publish an exciting range of travel, current affairs, biography, and popular science books as well. Our renewed focus on popular fiction is evident in our new titles by a host of fresh young talent from India and abroad. Jaico's recently established Translations Division translates selected English content into nine regional languages.

In addition to being a publisher and distributor of its own titles, Jaico is a major national distributor of books of leading international and Indian publishers. With its headquarters in Mumbai, Jaico has branches and sales offices in Ahmedabad, Bangalore, Bhopal, Chennai, Delhi, Hyderabad, Kolkata and Lucknow.

SINCE 1946